THIS IS NOT PARIS

BIS

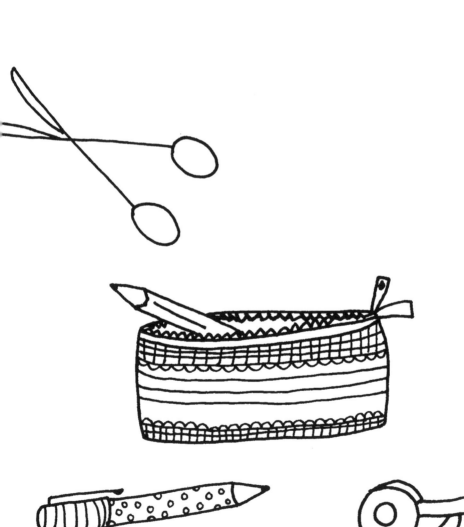

THIS BOOK BELONGS TO

DATE

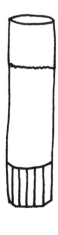

LA VIE, C'EST PARIS

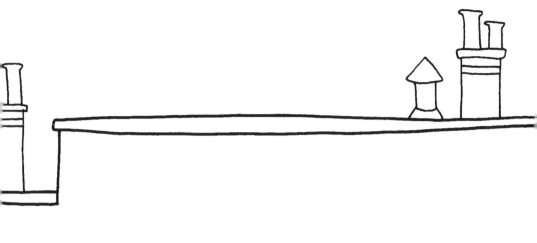

ARIS, C'EST LA VIE!

MARIE BASHKIRTSEFF

Things I would like to see and do in Paris

MARKERS, PENS, PENCILS & TUBES OF PAINT

LAVRUT
52 Passage Choiseul
75002 Paris (2e arr.)

ROUGIER&PLÉ
13-15 Boulevard des Filles du Calvaire
75003 Paris (3e arr.)

ADAM MONTPARNASSE
11 Boulevard Edgar Quinet
75014 Paris (14e arr.)

MAGASIN SENNELIER
3 Quai Voltaire
75007 Paris (7e arr.)

LE GÉANT DES BEAUX-ARTS
166 Rue de la Roquette
75011 Paris (11e arr.)

PASSAGE CLOUTÉ
7 Rue des Boulets
75011 Paris (11e arr.)

BOESNER
46 Rue du Chemin Vert
75011 Paris (11e arr.)

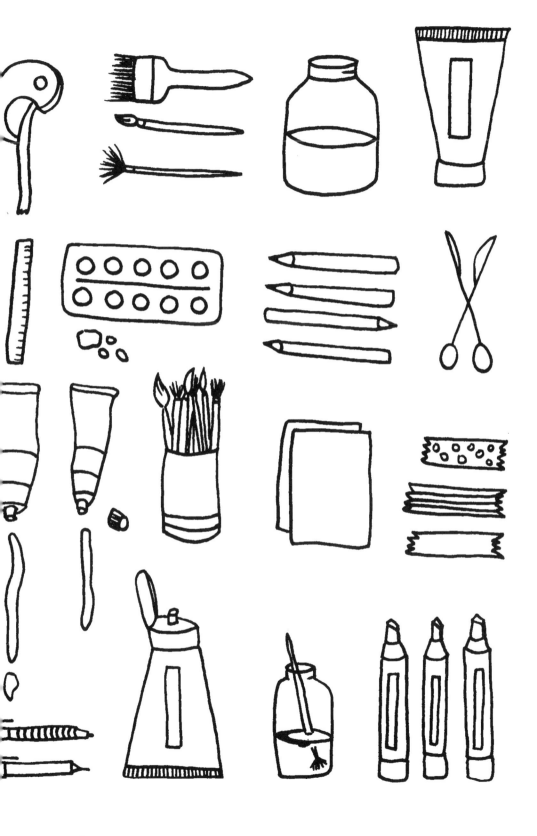

MÉTRO FOR PROS

Ⓜ ⓇⒺⓇ Ⓣ

Draw from the example of an actual metro map: which metro have you taken, where did you get off, and what are the most beautiful names?

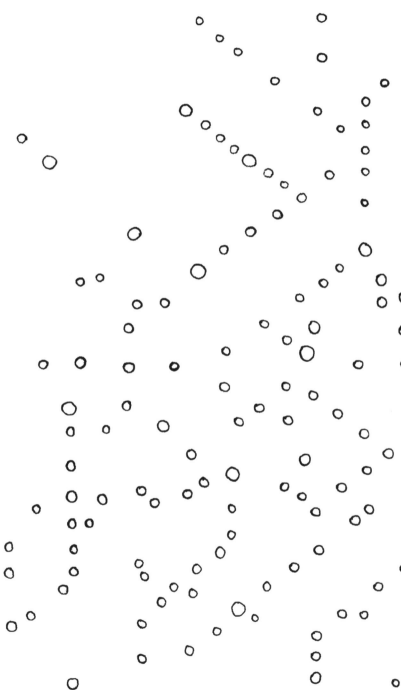

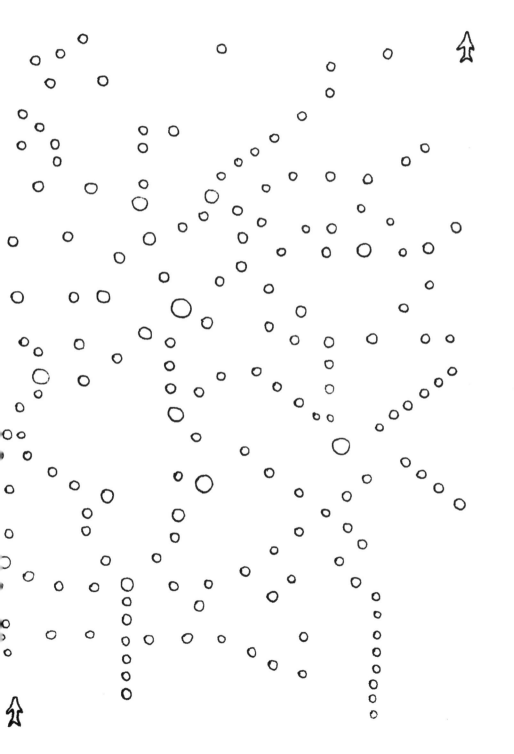

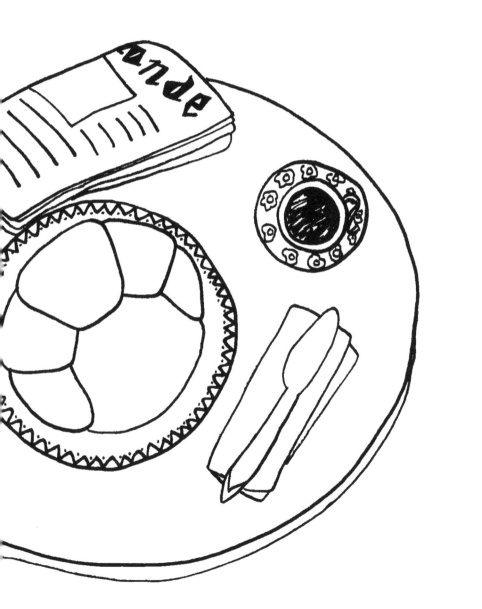

UN CAFÉ AU LAIT, S'IL VOUS PLAÎT

5X CLASSIC VENUES

☐ **CAFÉ DE FLORE**
172 Boulevard Saint-Germain
75006 Paris (6e arr.)

☐ **LES DEUX MAGOTS**
6 Place Saint-Germain-des-Prés
75006 Paris (6e arr.)

☐ **CAFÉ DE LA PAIX**
5 Place de l'Opéra
75009 Paris (9e arr.)

☐ **CAFÉ TOURNON**
18 Rue Tournon
75006 Paris (6e arr.)

☐ **CAFÉ DES DEUX MOULINS**
15 Rue Lepic
75018 Paris (18e arr.)

☐ ....
☐ ....
☐ ....

5X HIP COFFEE

☐ **COUTUME**
47 Rue de Babylone
75007 Paris (7e arr.)

☐ **TÉLESCOPE**
5 Rue Villedo
75001 Paris (1e arr.)

☐ **TEN BELLES**
10 Rue de la Grange aux Belles
75010 Paris (10e arr.)

☐ **CAFÉ KITSUNÉ**
51 Galerie de Montpensier
75001 Paris (1e arr.)

☐ **FRAGMENTS**
76 Rue des Tournelles
75003 Paris (3e arr.)

☐ ....
☐ ....
☐ ....

TICKETS & BUSINESS CARDS

Add your most beautiful ones to this
page, or copy them in a drawing.

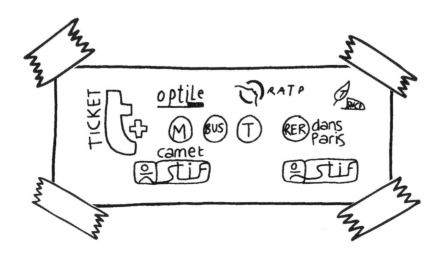

PARC DE LA VILLETTE

It's located a bit outside the centre, but the Parc de la Villette at the edge of the 19th arr. is an interesting park, offering more than just green patches and lots of trees. There is a cinema, a concert venue, a scientific museum with a huge reflecting ball and a music complex. The park is home to 26 bright red buildings, referred to as Folies and designed by the architect Bernard Tschumi.
Why don't you draw number 27?

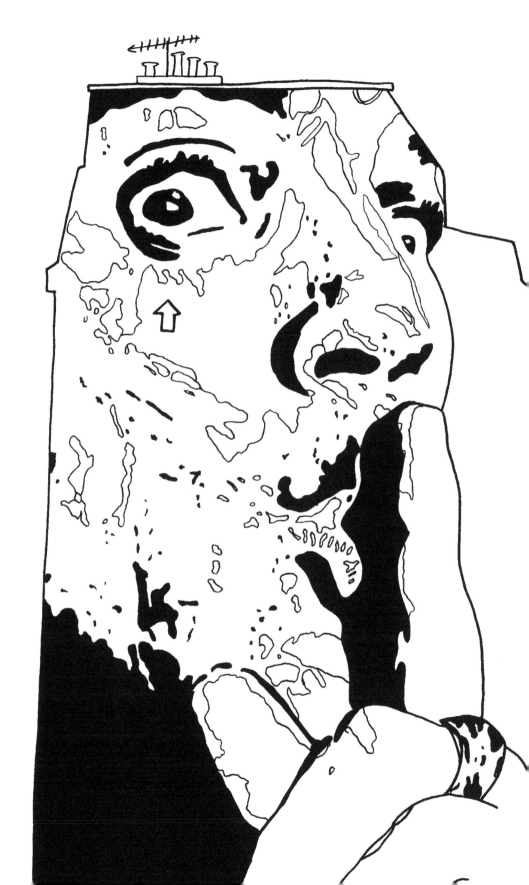

WITH OR WITHOUT BUBBLES

Still or sparkling? If you ask the Parisians, they will opt for sparkling water. Many litres are consumed on an annual basis. Fortunately, most brands of water are also available in environment-friendly glass bottles.

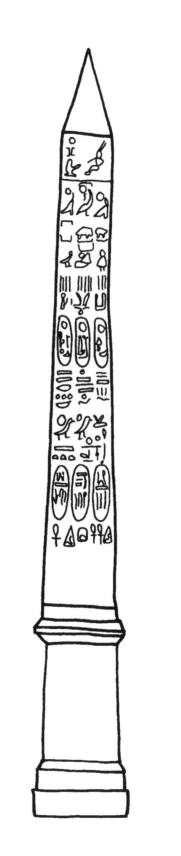

SIGHTS YOU DO NOT WANT TO MISS

Obviously, you don't have to go, but these highlights are popular for a reason. Tick off the place you have visited.

- [ ] NOTRE-DAME DE PARIS
- [ ] EIFFEL TOWER
- [ ] SACRÉ-COEUR
- [ ] ARC DE TRIOMPHE
- [ ] PLACE DES VOSGES
- [ ] OPÉRA GARNIER
- [ ] GALERIE VIVIENNE
- [ ] MONTMARTRE
- [ ] PÈRE-LACHAISE CEMETERY
- [ ] DÔME DES INVALIDES
- [ ] PANTHÉON
- [ ] SAINTE-CHAPELLE
- [ ] AVENUE DES CHAMPS-ÉLYSÉES
- [ ] PONT NEUF
- [ ] ÎLE DE LA CITÉ
- [ ] LA MADELEINE
- [ ] TOUR SAINT-JACQUES
- [ ] PROMENADE PLANTÉE
- [ ] PLACE VENDÔME
- [ ] ....
- [ ] ....
- [ ] ....

FLOWERS, LEAVES & SHOPPING LISTS

Add your most beautiful finds to this page.

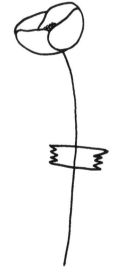

MOUSSE AU CHOCOLAT

Baba au rhum, *île flottante*, not only do French deserts have beautiful names, they often taste divine as well. One that you can quickly make yourself is chocolate mousse. Delicious after a meal, together with a hot cup of coffee. For 5-6 people.

300 gr. dark chocolate (at least 70% cocoa)
3 egg whites
200 ml cream
sea salt, preferably flakes (e.g. fleur de sel)
or coarse ground (e.g. Baleine)

Break 250 gr. of the chocolate into pieces, and keep the rest for the garnish. Melt the chocolate in a bowl hanging over a pan with gently boiling water (bain-marie). Do not allow the bowl to touch the water and keep stirring thoroughly.

Take the bowl off the fire as soon as the chocolate has melted. In a clean, grease-free bowl, beat the egg whites until stiff. In another bowl, beat the whipped cream until thick. Using a spatula, first fold the egg whites and subsequently the whipped cream into the chocolate. Divide between 5-6 bowls or glasses and leave to set in the refrigerator for at least 1 hour. Grate or shave the remaining chocolate on top and sprinkle with a pinch of sea salt.

Also delicious with some dried chilli pepper flakes instead of sea salt.

PLACE DE LA RÉPUBLIQUE

**Is located exactly on the border of the 3rd, 10th and 11th arrondissements.
Frequently the centre of demonstrations in the city.**

Of course, the statue on the square is many times more interesting than the square itself.
The sculpture, which was placed there in 1883, is the symbol of the important French motto: *liberté, egalité, fraternité* (liberty, equality, fraternity).

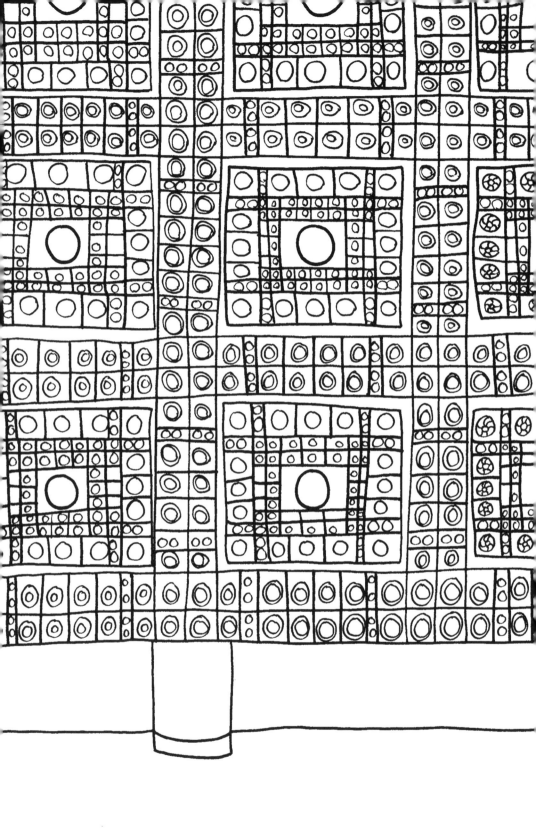

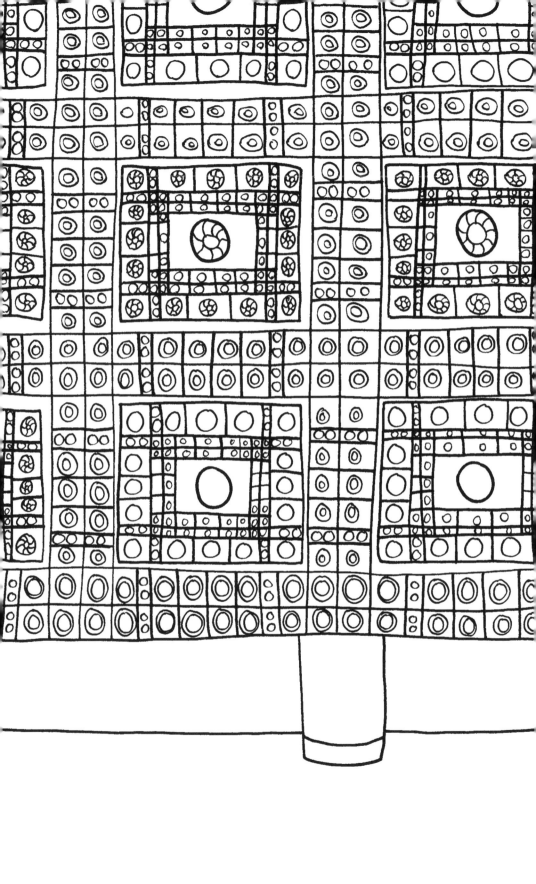

TIME FOR AN APÉRO!

You are not likely to meet any Parisians who never drink red wine. But without a plate of food? *Mais non.* Wine is meant to accompany the meal, and before dinner one enjoys an aperitif. Refer to your aperitif as your *apéro* and you will fully blend in with the French.

So no wine. However, champagne is allowed! Or Kir (Royal), beer from the tap (*pression*) or a cocktail. Utterly French is of course an *anisette*; an anise liqueur from the brands Ricard or Pernod, diluted with water. A small snack with your *apéro* is fully permitted: nuts, salty crisps or a tiny starter.

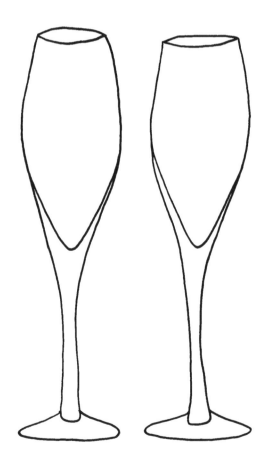

20 DISTRICTS (ARRONDISSEMENTS)

Officially, the districts of Paris are only given a number, which means their names are just nicknames. Together the numbers form a spiral, running from the centre outwards and clockwise. Each arrondissement has been divided into four *quartiers* or quarters. The postal code of any address indicates in which of the 20 districts you find yourself.

Where have you spent the night, or - a rather more fun question - where would you like to have your own 20 m2?

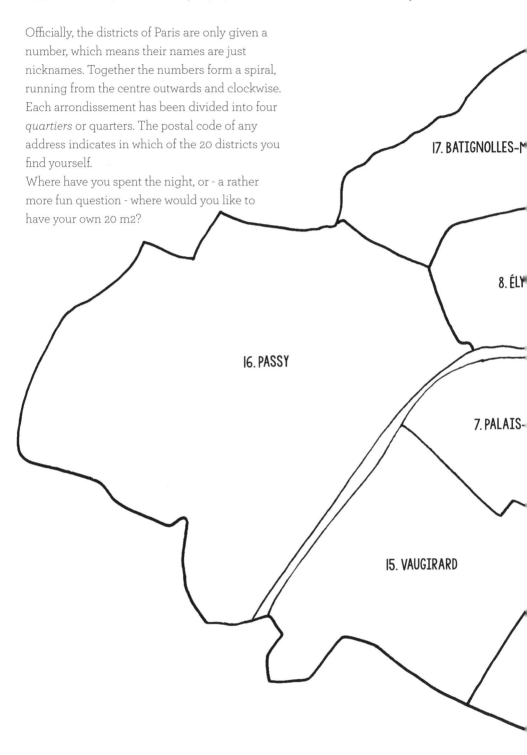

17. BATIGNOLLES-M

8. ÉLY

16. PASSY

7. PALAIS-

15. VAUGIRARD

Dreams, notes, ideas, discoveries

THE MOST BEAUTIFUL MUSEUMS

There are more than 150 museums in Paris - and that's not even including the galleries. These 11 are in any case highly worth your while.

THE 4 MOST FAMOUS ONES

- ☐ MUSÉE DU LOUVRE
  www.louvre.fr

- ☐ MUSÉE D'ORSAY
  www.musee-orsay.fr

- ☐ LE CENTRE POMPIDOU
  www.centrepompidou.fr

- ☐ MUSÉE RODIN
  www.musee-rodin.fr

- ☐ ....

- ☐ ....

- ☐ ....

PLUS 7 EXTRAORDINARY ONES

- ☐ CITÉ DES SCIENCES ET DE L'INDUSTRIE
  www.cite-sciences.fr

- ☐ MUSÉE DU QUAI BRANLY
  www.quaibranly.fr

- ☐ MUSÉE CARNAVALET
  www.carnavalet.paris.fr

- ☐ LE PETIT PALAIS
  www.petitpalais.paris.fr

- ☐ MUSÉE GOURMAND DU CHOCOLAT
  www.museeduchocolat.fr

- ☐ PALAIS DE TOKYO
  www.palaisdetokyo.com

- ☐ JEU DE PAUME
  www.jeudepaume.org

- ☐ ....

- ☐ ....

- ☐ ....

TUILERIES GARDEN

This large park in the 1st arr. is mainly known for its basins in which you can sail small boats. Fun for children, indeed, but the coloured miniature sailing ships, lazily going round in circles, are also wonderfully peaceful to watch for adults.

And as soon as you've had enough, you can admire sculptures by Auguste Rodin, Henry Moore, Roy Lichtenstein and many others in the park.

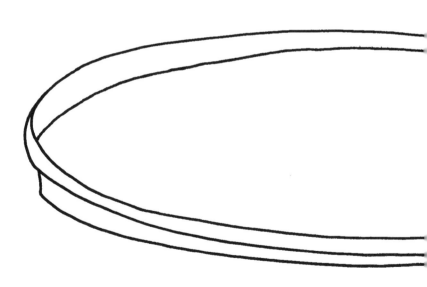

BISTROS & CLASSIC CUISINE

The dictionary indicates: a bistro, or *bistrot*, is an informal dining establishment, in between a bar and a restaurant. We say: a bistro is a marvellous institute and a weekend in Paris is not complete without a visit to one. Ordering meat can never go wrong if you memorise the following: *bleu* is rare, *saignant* is in between rare and medium, *à point* is what we call medium and *bien cuit* is, well, a waste of good meat: well-done.

WHERE?

LE BIDOU
12 Rue Anatole de la Forge
75017 Paris (17e arr.)

LE CHARDENOUX
1 Rue Jules Vallès
75011 Paris (11e arr.)

BOUILLON CHARTIER
7 Rue du Faubourg Montmartre
75009 Paris (9e arr.)

ALLARD
41 Rue Saint-André des Arts
75006 Paris (6e arr.)

LE CHATEAUBRIAND
129 Avenue Parmentier
75011 Paris (11e arr.)

....

....

WHAT?

- STEAK TARTARE
- ESCARGOTS À LA BOURGUIGNONNE
- SOUPE À L'OIGNON GRATINÉE
- MOULES-FRITES
- STEAK-FRITES
- MAGRET DE CANARD À L'ORANGE
- PLATEAU D'HUÎTRES
- SOLE MEUNIÈRE

....

....

EIFFEL TOWER

If you stand below the Eiffel Tower, precisely in the middle, and then look up, you will surely get a bit dizzy. That might also happen upon reading the numbers that go with the steel tower. Over 18,000 pieces of metal, 2.5 million rivets, a construction team of 500 people, 324 metres high. We actually find the number of people that have visited the Eiffel Tower even more staggering: 250 million.

MARCHÉ AUX PUCES

Is there anything more fun than visiting a flea market on the weekend? The Parisian markets are excellent for finding glassware and crockery, Pernod decanters, mirrors, taxidermy animals, chairs, and so on. Most of the markets are located on or just off the Boulevard Périphérique. The touristic Puces Saint-Ouen is a huge market that consists of a great number of smaller markets, each with their own character.

▢ **PUCES DE SAINT-OUEN**
138-140 Rue des Rosiers
93400 Saint-Ouen
www.marcheauxpuces-saintouen.com
www.paris-flea-market.com

▢ **PUCES DE VANVES**
Avenue Georges-Lafenestre / Avenue Marc-Sangnier
75014 Paris (14e arr.)
pucesdevanves.typepad.com

▢ **PUCES DE MONTREUIL**
Avenue du Professeur André Lemierre
75020 Paris (20e arr.)

▢ **PUCES D'ALIGRE**
Place d'Aligre
75012 Paris (12e arr.)
pucesaligre.unblog.fr

▢ ....

▢ ....

▢ ....

The city, the people, the sounds, the smells

FILMS IN, ABOUT & FROM PARIS

- [ ] HÔTEL DU NORD
- [ ] LAST TANGO IN PARIS
- [ ] INTOUCHABLES
- [ ] MIDNIGHT IN PARIS
- [ ] LE FABULEUX DESTIN D'AMÉLIE POULAIN
- [ ] RATATOUILLE
- [ ] LES AVENTURES EXTRAORDINAIRES D'ADÈLE BLANC-SEC
- [ ] LE WEEK-END
- [ ] BEFORE SUNSET
- [ ] THE LAST METRO
- [ ] LA DISCRÈTE
- [ ] GAINSBOURG (VIE HÉROÏQUE)
- [ ] 2 DAYS IN PARIS
- [ ] ....
- [ ] ....
- [ ] ....

CHANSONS & ROCK ETC.

- ☐ FRANCE GALL
- ☐ ÉDITH PIAF
- ☐ JOHNNY HALLYDAY
- ☐ BEN L'ONCLE SOUL
- ☐ BB BRUNES
- ☐ JULIEN CLERC
- ☐ CHRISTOPHE MAÉ
- ☐ PATRICK BRUEL
- ☐ DAVID GUETTA
- ☐ SERGE GAINSBOURG
- ☐ ....
- ☐ ....
- ☐ ....

DÉFENSE DE STATIONNER

Driving through Paris with a car means driving at great speed, honking the horn regularly and keeping a cool head. After all, the greatest test is yet to come: finding a parking spot. The best-known traffic sign in the city has to be *défense the Stationner*, which means parking prohibited. Thankfully, small cars are easily jammed into small spaces.

ATTENTION À LA MARCHE EN DESCENDANT DU TRAIN

At which stops did you get off? Highlight them here!

Abbesses
Alésia
Alexandre Dumas
Alma-Marceau
Anatole France
Anvers
Argentine
Arts et Métiers
Asnières-Gennevilliers-Les Courtilles
Assemblée Nationale
Aubervilliers-Pantin-Quatre Chemins
Avenue Émile Zola
Avron
Bagneux
Balard
Barbès-Rochechouart
Basilique de Saint-Denis
Bastille
Bel-Air
Belleville
Bérault
Bercy
Bibliothèque François Mitterrand
Billancourt
Bir-Hakeim
Blanche
Bobigny-Pablo Picasso
Boissière
Bolivar
Bonne Nouvelle
Botzaris
Boulogne-Jean Jaurès
Boulogne-Pont de Saint-Cloud
Boucicaut
Bourse
Bréguet-Sabin
Brochant
Buttes Chaumont
Buzenval
Cadet
Cambronne
Campo Formio
Cardinal Lemoine
Carrefour Pleyel
Censier-Daubenton
Champs-Élysées-Clemenceau
Chardon Lagache

Charenton-Écoles
Charles de Gaulle-Étoile
Charles Michels
Charonne
Château d'Eau
Château de Vincennes
Château-Landon
Château Rouge
Châtelet
Châtillon-Montrouge
Chaussée d'Antin-La Fayette
Chemin Vert
Chevaleret
Cité
Cluny-La Sorbonne
Colonel Fabien
Commerce
Concorde
Convention
Corentin Cariou
Corentin Celton
Corvisart
Cour Saint-Émillion
Courcelles
Couronnes
Créteil-L'Échat
Créteil-Préfecture
Créteil-Université
Crimée
Croix de Chavaux
Danube
Daumesnil
Denfert-Rochereau
Dugommier
Dupleix
Duroc
École Militaire
École Vétérinaire de Maisons-Alfort
Edgar Quinet
Église de Pantin
Esplanade de La Défense
Étienne Marcel
Europe
Exelmans
Faidherbe-Chaligny
Falguière
Félix Faure
Filles du Calvaire
Fort d'Aubervilliers
Franklin D. Roosevelt

Gabriel Péri
Gaîté
Gallieni
Gambetta
Gare d'Austerlitz
Gare de l'Est
Gare de Lyon
Gare du Nord
George V
Glacière
Goncourt
Grands Boulevards
Guy Môquet
Havre-Caumartin
Hoche
Hôtel de Ville
Invalides
Jacques Bonsergent
Jasmin
Jaurès
Javel – André Citroën
Jourdain
Jules Joffrin
Jussieu
Kléber
La Chapelle
La Courneuve-8 Mai 1945
La Défense-Grande Arche
La Fourche
La Motte-Picquet-Grenelle
La Muette
La Tour-Maubourg
Lamarck-Caulaincourt
Laumière
Le Kremlin-Bicêtre
Le Peletier
Ledru-Rollin
Les Agnettes
Les Gobelins
Les Halles
Les Sablons
Liberté
Liège
Louis Blanc
Louise Michel
Lourmel
Louvre-Rivoli
Mabillon
Madeleine
Mairie d'Issy
Mairie d'Ivry
Mairie de Clichy

Mairie de Montreuil
Mairie de Montrouge
Mairie de Saint-Ouen
Mairie des Lilas
Maison Blanche
Maisons-Alfort-Les Juilliottes
Maisons-Alfort-Stade
Malakoff-Plateau de Vanves
Malakoff-Rue Étienne Dolet
Malesherbes
Maraîchers
Marcadet-Poissonniers
Marcel Sembat
Marx Dormoy
Maubert-Mutualité
Ménilmontant
Michel Bizot
Michel-Ange-Auteuil
Michel-Ange-Molitor
Mirabeau
Miromesnil
Monceau
Montgallet
Montparnasse-Bienvenüe
Mouton-Duvernet
Nation
Nationale
Notre-Dame-de-Lorette
Notre-Dame-des-Champs
Oberkampf
Odéon
Olympiades
Opéra
Ourcq
Palais Royal-Musée du Louvre
Parmentier
Passy
Pasteur
Pelleport
Père Lachaise
Pereire
Pernety
Philippe Auguste
Picpus
Pierre et Marie Curie
Pigalle
Place d'Italie
Place de Clichy

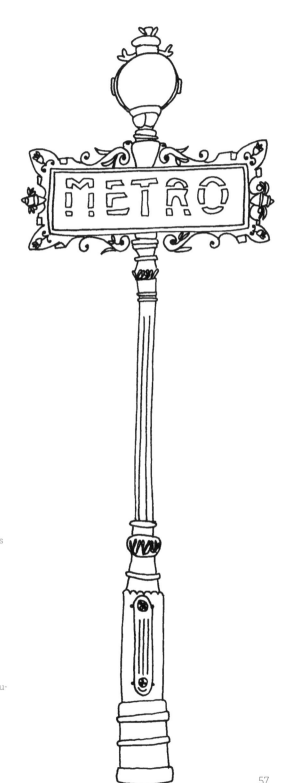

CREAKING BED & FLOWERY WALLPAPER

You must experience this at least once in your lifetime. A pink hotel room with flower patterns everywhere: from the wallpaper to the pillows to the bedspread and the painting. And an old bed with creaking springs. One of those beds in which you wake up halfway through the night, pressed together because you both rolled towards the dent in the middle. Nothing says romance like an old Parisian hotel.

TODAY WE DO NOTHING!

THEATRE & OPERA

'Great is the fortune of he who possesses a good bottle, a good book, and a good friend' according to Molière. Also quite nice: an evening out in one of the many splendid theatres and opera houses in Paris. Or visit a beautiful cinema. For colouring: the painting by Marc Chagall on the ceiling of the Palais Garnier.

☐ OPÉRA NATIONAL DE PARIS - PALAIS GARNIER
8 Rue Scribe, 75009 Paris (9e arr.)
www.operadeparis.fr

☐ OPÉRA NATIONAL DE PARIS - OPÉRA BASTILLE
Place de la Bastille, 75012 Paris (12e arr.)
www.operadeparis.fr

☐ LE LUCERNAIRE
53 Rue Notre-Dame des Champs, 75006 Paris (6e arr.)
www.lucernaire.fr

☐ LE CINÉMATHÈQUE FRANÇAISE
51 Rue de Bercy, 75012 Paris
www.cinematheque.fr

☐ THÉÂTRE MONTPARNASSE
31 Rue de la Gaîté, 75014 Paris (14e arr.)
www.theatremontparnasse.com

☐ THÉÂTRE DU ROND-POINT
2bis Avenue Franklin D. Roosevelt, 75008 Paris (8e arr.)
www.theatredurondpoint.fr

☐ ....

☐ ....

☐ ....

BASILIQUE DU SACRÉ-COEUR

**First stone laid in 1875.
Can be reached by means of 222
steps or the Montmartre
funicular.**

A bright white church on top of the
hill, built to commemorate the
thousands of casualties during the
French-German war. Nowadays, the
Sacré-Coeur is a bustling meeting
point with a beautiful view of the
city. Amidst the 11 million visitors
per year, it is also the peaceful place
of residence of sixteen Benedictine
sisters.

Spots I have visited and wish to remember

MOULIN ROUGE

Huge skirts with lots of lace, French cancan music, ladies with large wigs, and legs swinging high up into the air. For at least 125 years, this cabaret theatre with its red mill on the roof has been the most famous in Paris. It is located on the Boulevard de Clichy in the 18th district. Big names that are associated with the Moulin Rouge: painter Henri de Toulouse-Lautrec, singer Édith Piaf and Yves Montand. The latter, an actor and singer who went on to become world-famous, once featured as Piaf's supporting act.

BUTTERFLIES, MAMMOTHS, BIRDS & FABLE ANIMALS

Since 1831, the extraordinary shop
Deyrolle in the Rue du Bac has
been selling pinned butterflies,
taxidermy animals, old skulls and
funny *créatures fantastiques*.
Not for sale, but just as impressive,
are the taxidermy animals in the
Galerie de paléontologie et
d'anatomie comparée at the Jardin
des Plantes.

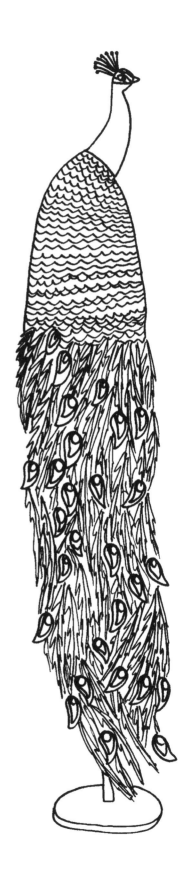

A PARTY WITHOUT A CAKE IS JUST A MEETING

JULIA CHILD

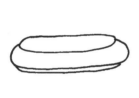

HOW TO DRESS
LIKE A PARISIAN

Ballerinas or high heels, but
nothing in between. Skinny jeans,
dark and without any funny holes.
Breton stripe jumper, dark jacket,
not too many pieces of jewellery,
understated make-up, large
sunglasses, messy hair.
Nothing to add.

BEAUTIFUL BOOKSHOPS

☐ **SHAKESPEARE AND COMPANY**
   37 Rue de la Bûcherie
   75005 Paris (5e arr.)

☐ **LIBRAIRIE GOURMANDE**
   92-96 Rue Montmartre
   75002 Paris (2e arr.)

☐ **LIBRAIRIE GALIGNANI**
   224 Rue de Rivoli
   75001 Paris (1e arr.)

☐ **ARTAZART DESIGN BOOKSTORE**
   83 Quai de Valmy
   75010 Paris (10e arr.)

☐ **OFR.**
   20 Rue Dupetit-Thouars
   75003 Paris (3e arr.)

☐ **LA HUNE**
   16-18 Rue de l'Abbaye
   75006 Paris (6e arr.)

☐ **LIBRAIRIE PHOTOGRAPHIQUE LE 29**
   29 Rue des Récollets
   75010 Paris (10e arr.)

☐ **LIBRAIRIE GALERIE LE MONTE-EN-L'AIR**
   71 Rue de Ménilmontant / 2 Rue de la Mare
   75020 Paris (20e arr.)

☐ **PARIS LIBRAIRIES**
   Over 90 independent bookshops in Paris
   www.parislibrairies.fr

☐

BOOKS ABOUT PARIS

- [ ] **ERNEST HEMINGWAY,** A Moveable Feast

- [ ] **ÉMILE ZOLA,** Nana

- [ ] **DAVID SEDARIS,** Me Talk Pretty One Day

- [ ] **VICTOR HUGO,** The Hunchback of Notre-Dame

- [ ] **DAVID LEBOVITZ,** The Sweet Life in Paris

- [ ] **CÉCILE DAVID-WEILL,** The Suitors

- [ ] **CAROLINE DE MAIGRET E.A.,** How to be Parisian Wherever You Are

- [ ] **A.J. LIEBLING,** Between Meals: An Appetite for Paris

- [ ] **RUSS RYMER,** Paris Twilight

- [ ] **HONORÉ DE BALZAC,** Illusions perdues

- [ ] **ALAIN DUCASSE,** J'aime Paris

- [ ] **MURIEL BARBERY,** The Elegance of the Hedgehog

- [ ] **EDMUND WHITE,** The Flâneur

- [ ] **TATIANA DE ROSNAY,** Elle s'appelait Sarah

- [ ] **DAN BROWN,** The Da Vinci Code

- [ ] ....

- [ ] ....

TALL PEOPLE, SHORT PEOPLE, FAT PEOPLE, SKINNY PEOPLE

Seen any intriguing people on the platform across from yours? Draw them!

NORD

COCO CHANEL

The inventor of 'the little black dress'
and the women's suit is the woman
who found that you can only be
beautiful if you decide to be yourself.
This progressive fashion designer
introduced Chanel No.5 to the market
in 1921 and the well-known
topstitched handbag with a chain
strap in the 1950s. Coco Chanel died
age 87, in style: in the Ritz Hotel on
the Place Vendôme.
Right around the corner from the
hotel, on Rue Cambon at number 31, a
Chanel shop can still be found at the
address where Coco Chanel opened
one of her first shops in 1918.

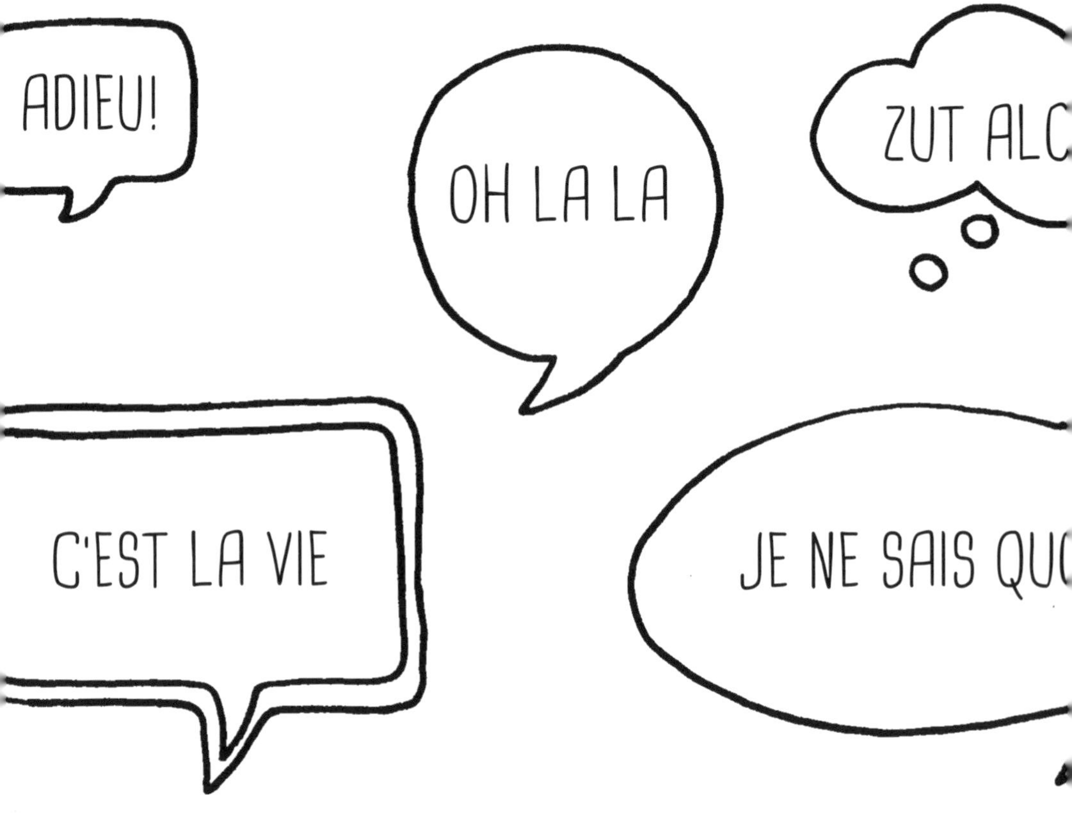
ADIEU!
OH LA LA
ZUT ALC
C'EST LA VIE
JE NE SAIS QU

OH LA LA

Those who do not speak any French and have to make do with English, will mix it up with a few French words every now and then. The English and Americans will have had a good reason for making this a habit.

BETTER THAN A
TEXT MESSAGE

Below, note down the names of five people, buy
five postcards and five stamps, and then write
five beautiful sentences on each card.
Do not forget to post.

KITSCH & ART

Take a picture of the ugliest
souvenirs you encounter and add
the photographs to this page.
Or draw them. Our favourite:
the snow globe with the
Eiffel Tower.

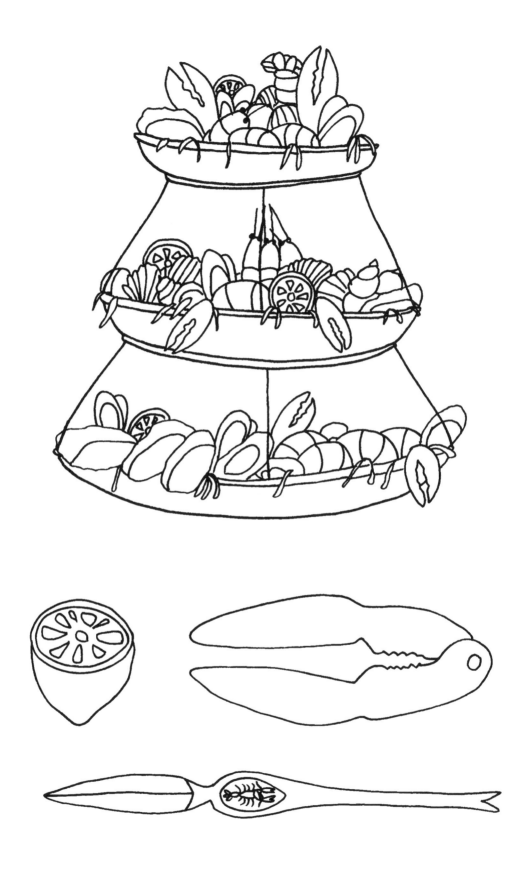

PLATEAU DE FRUITS DE MER

For an authentic *plateau de fruits de mer* it is important that you go to a good fish vendor and buy very fresh, tasty fish and shellfish. Drink fresh white wine or champagne with it. The quantities outlined below are for 4 people. Roughly.

3 litres tasty vegetable stock
8 langoustines
250 gr. periwinkles
250 gr. unpeeled grey shrimps
250 gr. cockles
500 gr. mussels
500 gr. crab claws, boiled
8-12 oysters
1 bag of crushed ice

Heat the stock and separately boil the langoustines (5 min.), the periwinkles (10 min.), and the shrimps (20 min.) and the cockles and the mussels. The shells are done as soon as they have opened. As soon as their done, scoop them out from the stock with a skimmer and set them aside. The crab claws will usually be sold ready-boiled. If you yourself are not all that skilful at opening oysters, you can let the fish vendor take care of that for you. Cover a large platter with crushed ice, divide the *fruits de mer* and put on the table. Serve with small bowls of lukewarm water with lemon, to clean your fingers in between eating. Also serve with: mayonnaise, vinaigrette of finely chopped red onion and wine vinegar and of course the necessary tools for opening the langoustines and the crab claws.

MY 8 MOST BEAUTIFUL PHOTOS

Print out on 5 x 5 cm stick them in.
Just like a real Polaroid!

BARGAINS & BAD BUYS

Regretting that one jacket you left behind? If only you could have just kept yourself from buying those expensive trousers.
Draw your bad buys, bargains and missed purchases here.

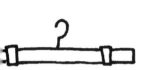 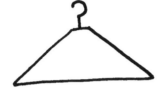 

ARC DE TRIOMPHE DE L'ÉTOILE

We always refer to the Arc de Triomphe, as if there weren't many more triumphal arches in France. Thus this one, on the Champs-Élysées in the 1st arrondissement, officially has a much longer name. On *Quatorze Juillet*, a national holiday, a huge flag is hung over the arch. The Arc de Triomphe is famous due to the grave of the unknown soldier hidden beneath it, but also thanks to many strange stunts performed at it: flying through the arch with a small airplane or frying an egg on the eternal flame.

ROOM WITH A VIEW

What do you see from your window: the Sacré-Coeur, the beautiful Parisian rooftops, the Notre-Dame or do you overlook a nice green park?

ENJOYED YOUR FOOD?

Copy your plate in a drawing, add the cards of the
nicest restaurants you visited, and photographs of
that pretty cake, that tasty piece of cheese...

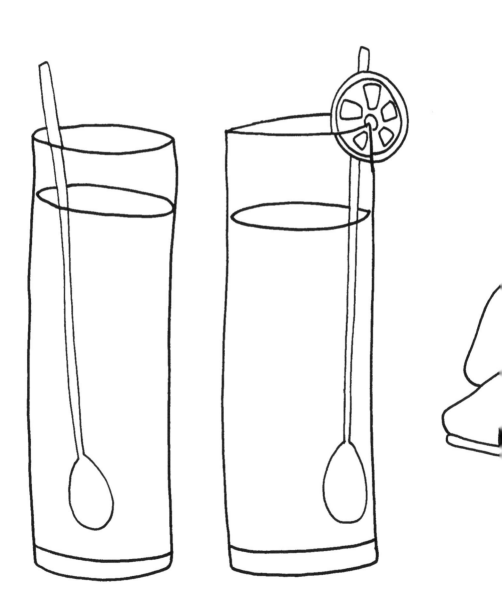

CITRON PRESSÉ

Long before drinking a glass of lukewarm water with lemon juice became so popular, the French – of course – already had their own version. With sugar or honey added, though. *Citron pressé* is a refreshing drink for summer days, when you get bored with water. It tastes good with ordinary still water, but sparkling water with light bubbles also works nicely. You need 1 lemon per person.

1 lemon couple of ice cubes
mineral water
sugar, honey or agave syrup
sprig of mint (optional)

Squeeze out the lemon. Add some ice cubes in a glass and pour the lemon juice in. Top up with mineral water, and add the sprig of mint, if so desired. You can add the sugar, honey or agave syrup to taste.

LE IT BAG

Although real Parisians would never want to be seen with eye-catching logos, the best-known designer bags come from Paris. The famous Birkin bag by Hermès, the round Speedy by Vuitton or the cheapest of all: Le Pliage by Longchamp. The odd one out is the much-loved Italian bag by Fendi with its quintessentially French name Baguette.

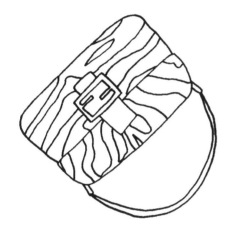

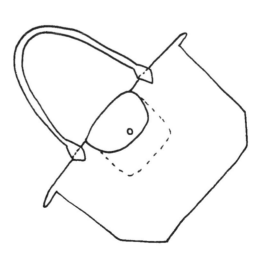

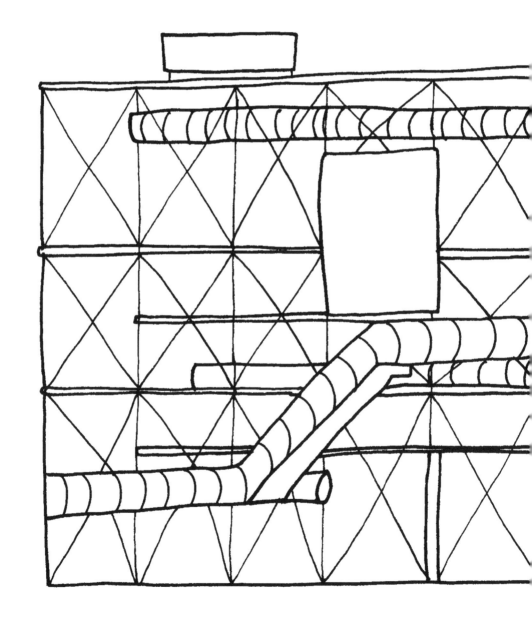

CENTRE GEORGES POMPIDOU

This building, with its many coloured pipes and the long escalator along its exterior appears to have been folded inside out, and that was exactly the effect intended by the architects. Once you get over your amazement, proceed to enter the building. Inside you will find a bookshop, a museum for modern art, galleries, a cinema and restaurants. All under one roof.

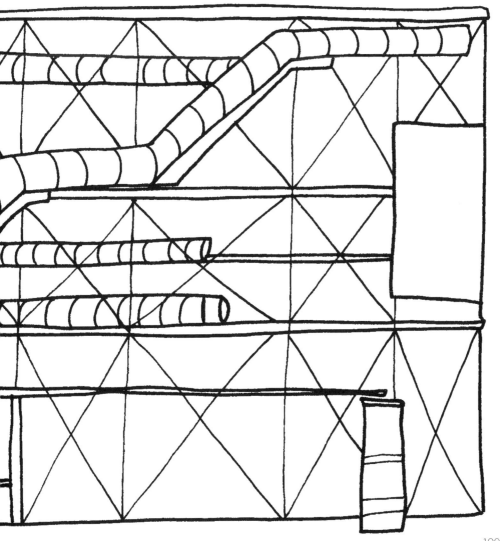

OVER THE PARISIAN ROOFTOPS

Draw the view from the Centre Georges Pompidou, the hills at the Sacré-Coeur, the Tour Montparnasse or the Parc des Buttes-Chaumont

SAY WHAT?

The French do speak quite civilised and softly, but perhaps you will succeed nonetheless: eavesdrop on conversations, very carefully, while you're sitting on a terrace, on a chair in the Jardin du Luxembourg or during a long ride on the metro.

Inspiration for at home, at work, on holidays, and the rest of my life

TYPICAL PARIS

Print out your photographs on 5 x 5
cm and add them here. Just like a real
Polaroid!

MUSÉE D'ORSAY

The *Mona Lisa* is on display in the
Louvre, but the Musée d'Orsay
offers many more splendid
portraits: by Gauguin, Manet,
Cézanne and numerous other
famous French painters.
Fun to copy in a drawing, or
simply fill the empty frames on
this page with your own portraits.

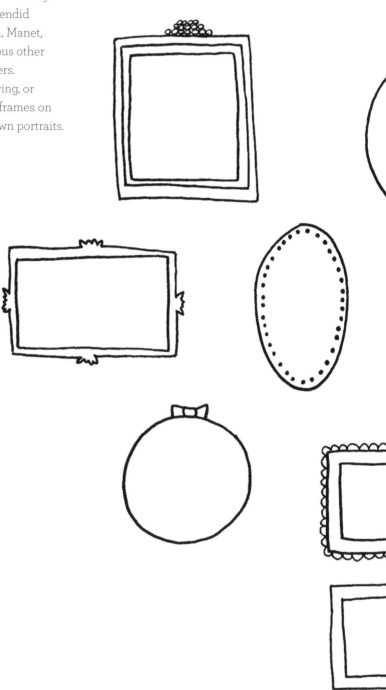

PHARMACIE

Polâine   Polâin

ES GRANDS MAGASINS

u can shop in one of the large well-known department stores, or look for a nice concept store
t also sells 'everything'.

X DEPARTMENT STORE

LE BON MARCHÉ RIVE GAUCHE
24 Rue de Sèvres
75007 Paris (7e arr.)

LE BHV MARAIS
52 Rue de Rivoli
75004 Paris (4e arr.)

GALERIES LAFAYETTE HAUSSMANN
40 Boulevard Haussmann
75009 Paris (9e arr.)

PRINTEMPS HAUSSMANN
64 Boulevard Haussmann
75009 Paris (9e arr.)

....

....

....

5X CONCEPT STORE

☐ MERCI
111 Boulevard Beaumarchais
75003 Paris (3e arr.)

☐ COLETTE
213 Rue Saint-Honoré
75001 Paris (1e arr.)

☐ CENTRE COMMERCIAL
2 Rue de Marseille
75010 Paris (10e arr.)

☐ THE COLLECTION
33 Rue de Poitou
75003 Paris (3e arr.)

☐ FRENCH TROTTERS
128 Rue Vieille du Temple
75003 Paris (3e arr.)

☐ ....

☐ ....

☐ ....

18 PAIRS OF SUNGLASSES, BEARDS, WILD HAIR, BERETS & SUMMER FRECKLES GET CREATIVE!

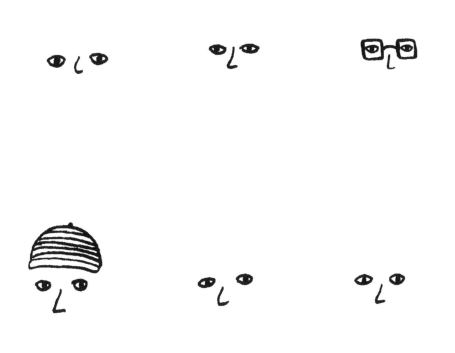

Next time I'm in Paris...

18-19 JEF AEROSOL A well-known French street artist is Jef Aerosol.
You will find this work *Chuuuttt!!!* near the Centre Pompidou on the Place Igor Stravinksy.

30-31 INSTITUT DU MONDE ARABE Institute for the distribution of knowledge on the Arab world, with its beautiful façade. In this building you will find, among other things, a restaurant and a museum.

50-51 BOUQUINISTES ALONG THE SEINE From the Pont Marie - Quay du Louvre on the Rive Gauche and in between the Quai de la Tournelle - Quai Malaquais on the opposite bank, you'll find over 200 bookshops in more than 900 green stalls.

86-87 CANAL SAINT-MARTIN In the summer this is one large picnic place, where hundreds of people sit along the water with a bottle of wine.

120-121 INDISPENSABLE SHOPS An imaginary street with the most important shops in the city: a pharmacy, a bar-tabac, a chocolatier that sells macarons (Ladurée) and an excellent baker (Poilâne)...

COLOPHON

ILLUSTRATIONS Anne van Haasteren
TEXT & COMPILATION Petra de Hamer
CO-AUTHOR Kim Snijders
DESIGN Oranje Vormgevers

THIS IS MY PARIS

isbn 978-90-6369-394-7

BISPUBLISHERS

© Text by Petra de Hamer and illustrated by Anne van Haasteren
© English edition: BIS Publishers, Amsterdam, July 2015
© Original edition: Uitgeverij Mo'Media bv, Breda, The Netherlands, www.momedia.nl

This publication has been compiled with the utmost care.
BIS Publishers cannot be held liable for any inadequacies in the text.
Any comments can be addressed to:
BIS Publishers, Building Het Sieraad, Postjesweg 1, 1057 DT Amsterdam.
info@bispublishers.nl, www.bispublishers.nl

ISBN 978-90-6369-394-7

9 789063 693947 >